BREATHING | ROOM

The space between our current pace and our limits

ANDY STANLEY

NORTH POINT
RESOURCES

CONTENTS

INTRODUCTION

A Problem-Loaded Word
by Andy Stanley

When I was growing up, we had a unique holiday "tradition." Every year between Christmas and New Year's, my dad would go down to the storage area of our basement and clean it out. He would take out bag after bag of things to throw away. He would carefully organize whatever was left, labeling everything and putting it all where it belonged. This would take him several days to accomplish, but he hated clutter, and he worked at it diligently.

When it was done, he would show it off to the family, navigating us through the beautiful order of it all. We all admired it.

Then, starting on January 1, my mom—who doesn't like to throw *anything* away—would begin undoing all his work, and she would keep at it for the rest of the year. We would also take stuff down there and drop it anywhere we liked. Anything anybody didn't know what to do with got tossed in the basement.

By the time the next Christmas rolled around, all evidence of my dad's organization had been buried in clutter—and so the "tradition" would start all over again.

Now, in my mom's defense (as if she needed any here), she's an artist, and that's just the way God made her. She thrives with stuff cluttered around her, just as God made my dad to thrive in an atmosphere of neatness and order.

No Room for Anything More

Maybe you've got a basement, spare room, attic, or car that looks like our basement did—so full of stuff you can hardly squeeze in another thing. It's easy to laugh about these cluttered spaces, whether our own or our neighbor's.

But how funny is it when someone's *life* looks like that? How humorous is it when a life is so jam-packed and on edge that there's no margin?

Let's ask ourselves some questions.

How much room is there in our schedules to add "extra" things that could be strongly beneficial—things that look healthy, enjoyable, and right?

How much room is there in our finances to afford it?

How much room is there in our relationships to fully and openly enjoy those new things with those who love us most and whom we love most?

If "not much" would have to be your answer to those questions, you know something's wrong. When there's no room in your life to squeeze anything else in, the situation becomes problematic. It's no fun when you're so stressed out—or you watch someone you love who is so stressed out—that relationships start to deteriorate, and enjoyment is lost.

Is There a Choice?

You may feel you don't have any choice about living this way, stressed to the max. You think, *That's just the way life is.* After all, you look around and everybody else's life looks the same way.

Or you tell yourself, *Well, it's just for this season—later it will all clear up and things will slow down.* But it never does. And deep inside, we know it never will, unless we make radical changes.

Here's something else we all know deep inside: at the end of the day, life is simply *better* with enough space to really breathe.

Breathing room means you actually have time to talk to the people in your family.

Breathing room is having dinner together around the table.

Breathing room means we don't have to drive eighty miles an

hour everywhere.

Breathing room means there's actually money left over at the end of the month.

Breathing room means we actually *enjoy* what we're doing—because we're not doing all the things we *could* be doing, or all the things everybody else is doing.

Breathing room means sitting quietly with others and being able to actually concentrate on what they're saying, because we aren't so distracted by everything we haven't gotten done.

Breathing room means going to church and being able to fully participate with your mind and heart.

Breathing room is being able to pray and actually focus on what you're praying about.

Life is better. I know I don't have to convince you of that.

So, we're going to talk about it in this study. And we're going to discover that God actually has something to say about all this.

Let's take a close look at this appealing idea of *finding room to breathe*—something that's appropriate and applicable for all of us.

SESSION 1

Ex-Squeeze Yourself

In your house, is there a closet or two stuffed so full that the whole mess might come crashing down if you try to cram in one more thing?

If so, that's *fine*. And *you're* fine. God made some of us to push toward neatness and organization, while others are comfortable with clutter and aren't really bothered by messes around them. God made us all different.

It's *okay* for your closets to be crammed and chaotic.

It's *not* okay for your life to be that way.

It's not okay for your schedule to be that way—where you're squeezed in by so much busyness, you can't fully take pleasure in any of it.

It's not okay for your finances to be that way—with no discretionary dollars and absolutely no room for error; the stress over this never lifts.

It's not okay for your relationships to be that way—where everyone's running in a dozen different directions, and you feel you hardly know what's really going on inside one another, and you rarely ever talk—*really* talk.

DISCUSSION STARTER

Do you like a neat, orderly, clutter-free life? Or are you at ease with lots of random stuff all around you? How does that preference affect your daily life? How does it relate to what your life is like overall, inwardly and outwardly?

VIDEO OVERVIEW

For Session 1 of the DVD

Breathing room is the space or the distance between our current pace and our limits. It applies to our schedules, our finances, and our relationships.

We all have limits. Though we all have different capacities, there comes a point when we just can't cram in anything more.

If you live at the edge of your limits, you stop enjoying the life God has given you to lead, and you lose control of your life. You trade peace for prosperity.

For the Christian, this is an issue of faith. Jesus has addressed these things directly. To be his followers, we must keep a sustainable pace.

When this breathing room is lacking, several things happen. Our stress levels rise, and our focus narrows, often in unhealthy ways. Consequently, our relationships suffer. We tune out what's most important and what brings true joy—our relationships. Happiness in life is measured by the health of our relationships, not by our prosperity or progress.

Why do we do this? Why do we push ourselves to the edge of our limits?

Fundamentally, a big part of what drives this for many of us is fear. None of us wants to be fearful, so it's hard to admit it.

What do we fear?

Some of us fear *missing out.*

We fear *falling behind.*

There's also a fear (especially for men) of *not mattering*, of failing to have our lives count for something. As progress-oriented people, we want to accomplish certain goals, and if we fail, we're afraid our lives lack meaning. Yet this fear of not mattering much has the potential to draw us away from what matters most.

Life is strange in the sense that we don't get to relive any part of our pasts. We get only one cycle through life; if we get it wrong, in the end we will have regrets.

But *what if we began to think differently?* What if we were willing to address our fears and to take an honest look at what drives our schedules, our spending, and our relationships?

In the Bible, God speaks to this issue in an unusual way. The Bible shows us again and again a contrast between fear and faith.

The issue has to do with how much we'll really *trust* God and his care for us.

For example, God's deep-rooted care for us was demonstrated in the Old Testament when God required his people to take one day off in every seven (the Sabbath). In this way, he built breathing room into their society.

Thus, God began to teach his people at the most elementary level about their need to trust him. God understands how we're wired, and he knows our need for breathing room.

VIDEO NOTES

_____

_____

_____

_____

_____

_____

_____

_____

_____

_____

_____

_____

_____

_____

_____

_____

_____

_____

_____

DISCUSSION QUESTIONS

1. As you observe your own life or the lives of those around you, when people operate very close to their limits, how does this affect them physically, emotionally, mentally, and relationally?

2. Where do you feel you need some breathing room? In what areas could you be living dangerously close to your limits, and how is this affecting you? What are the forces at work in your life that tend to push you toward these limits? To what degree is *fear* involved in this?

3. How fully conscious are you of the fact that God knows your personal limits in every area of life? How does this fact affect your ability to trust him?

4. Jesus reminds us (in Mark 2:27) that God gave the Sabbath for man's benefit. In Exodus 20:8–11, look at how the Sabbath is described in this listing of God's Ten Commandments. What does this reveal about God's care for humanity and his understanding of humanity? What else does it reveal about his character?

5. Look also at the provision God made for his people in Leviticus 19:9–10 (and extended further in Deuteronomy 24:19–22). What does this provision reveal about God's character? What practical benefit would this have provided? How does the principle here relate to the concept of finding breathing room in our lives today?

6. Finally, look at the words of Jesus in Matthew 6:25–33. What good reasons for trusting God do you find here? How does this passage expose our fears? In the practical matters of life, what does trusting God really look like, according to the guidelines given in this passage?

MILEPOSTS

- It's *not* okay for our lives to be so packed and fast-paced and stretched to our limits that we have no breathing room.

- We *all* have limits.

- We often push ourselves to the edge of our limits because of our fears.

MOVING FORWARD

No matter what you do, you're going to live within limits—the limits culture drives you to, the limits fear places upon you . . . or the limits your heavenly Father will lead you to. What's at stake isn't your progress; it's your *peace*.

CHANGING YOUR MIND

Listen carefully to these words of Jesus. Reflect especially on the amazing love our heavenly Father has for us, which is conveyed through what his Son tells us here:

> *So do not worry, saying, "What shall we eat?"*
> *or "What shall we drink?" or "What shall we wear?"*
> *For the pagans run after all these things,*
> *and your heavenly Father knows that you need them.*
> *But seek first his kingdom and his righteousness,*
> *and all these things will be given to you as well.*
> *Therefore do not worry about tomorrow,*
> *for tomorrow will worry about itself.*
> *Each day has enough trouble of its own.*
> *Matthew 6:31–34*

PREPARATION FOR SESSION 2

To help you prepare for Session 2, use these suggested devotions during the week leading up to your small group meeting.

Day One

Read Psalm 90, which was written by Moses. Reflect carefully on the first six verses. How would you explain in your own words what these verses tell us about God? What do they tell us about humanity?

Day Two

In Psalm 90:7–11, what further truths does Moses call attention to regarding humanity's condition? Why are these truths important for human beings to grasp?

Day Three

Reflect deeply on verse 12 in Psalm 90. What does it mean, practically, for you to "number your days"? What would it mean to possess "a heart of wisdom"?

Day Four

Read the words Moses prays in Psalm 90:13–15. How do these verses demonstrate a wise perspective on life?

Day Five

Reflect on the final two verses in Psalm 90, as the prayer of Moses concludes. How would you express this prayer in your own words?

Last Session

Chronically living our lives to the limits—and we *all* have limits—is damaging to our peace and happiness. We are meant to have *breathing room*. Yet our fears often keep us from accepting that.

SESSION 2

Time

When God established the nation of Israel and gave them rules for this new society, one thing he commanded them to do was to take a day off each week.

God was saying, "I've designed you to function best when there's *room to breathe* in your schedule." We were created for breathing room.

But our inclination is to keep forcing more things into our schedules while taking nothing out. Our tendency is to *do* so much that we end up enjoying very little of it.

This over-busyness reveals itself when we're constantly telling people, "I might be there fifteen minutes late," or "I may have to leave a few minutes early." We're driving too fast, and we're eating in the car. At work, we're thinking about what we need to get done at home; at home, we're worrying over what needs to happen at work.

Everything's always go, go, go. We feel we've got to work it all in so we can work it all out—yet we never get close to achieving that.

To address this problem, we'll look at one big idea with one application that could change your life. That's because *it will change your time* . . . and your time *is* your life.

DISCUSSION STARTER

Many have said that our culture effectively shuts out the idea of death, practically denying its existence. Do you sense this to be true? If so, how has this cultural norm affected your own thinking? How often do you find yourself thinking about your death? In what ways do you think of it?

VIDEO OVERVIEW

For Session 2 of the DVD

Moses' wisdom grew out of the four very different parts of his life— each one a life of its own.

First, as a young Hebrew, he was raised as an Egyptian in Pharaoh's household.

Later as a man, after earning Pharaoh's disfavor, he left Egypt and served as a shepherd for forty years.

In the third part of his life, he was back in Egypt for one of the biggest events in world history. He faced down Pharaoh and led God's people out of slavery.

Finally, he was the leader of this new nation of Israel for forty years as they wandered in the wilderness toward the Promised Land.

To enlighten our perspective on time, we find wisdom from this same Moses in one of the psalms he wrote, Psalm 90. Here he gives us a context for every decision we make concerning how we use our time.

In this psalm, Moses presents the everlastingness of God as the overarching context of Israel's life as a nation.

He reminds us that God controls the beginning and the end of our lives. Most of us do indeed believe that God has something to do with how long we live.

Moses reminds us that the magnitude of God's existence dwarfs the brevity of our lives. Moses suggests that if we could see God as he is, we would give him the reverence he is due—and we would be more careful with the time we've been allotted.

The true context for evaluating our lives is the recognition that God is "from everlasting to everlasting" (Psalm 90:2). This will directly impact what we decide to do with our time.

Moses asks God to teach us to live as if our days are numbered. This isn't depressing; it's reality.

Then comes the promise: Moses says that by numbering our days in this way, "we may gain a heart of wisdom" (90:12). That includes wisdom for setting priorities and avoiding regret.

Our time is limited—so we need to limit how we spend it.

VIDEO NOTES

_____

_____

_____

_____

_____

_____

_____

_____

_____

_____

_____

_____

_____

_____

_____

_____

_____

_____

_____

_____

DISCUSSION QUESTIONS

1. What are the biggest lessons you've learned about spending time wisely?

2. To what degree do you view time as your most treasured asset? On a practical level, what does it look like for a person to truly regard time as his or her most treasured asset?

3. What are the most significant pressures you face as you try to make wise decisions about your use of time? How can you counteract these pressures?

4. One recent researcher (Bronnie Ware of Australia, in her book *The Top Five Regrets of the Dying* published in 2012) identified these top two deathbed regrets: (1) "I wish I'd had the courage to live a life true to myself, not the life others expected of me," and (2) "I wish I hadn't worked so hard" (this one being especially common among men). How would you evaluate your life in those two areas? How likely is it that either of those regrets will be in your own mind as you lie upon your deathbed?

5. How fully does your current schedule allow you to pursue what you know is truly most important in your life? Who or what do you need to *add* to your schedule, or give more time to? Who or what do you need to *remove* from your schedule, or give less time to?

6. When you give serious thought to making your schedule align more closely with your deepest values and priorities, what fears or anxieties come to mind?

MILEPOSTS

- Your time *is* your life.

- The right context for viewing our time is the everlastingness of God and the brevity of our earthly existence.

- The Bible instructs us to keep the perspective that our days are limited, and, therefore, to make our time-use decisions in light of that.

MOVING FORWARD

Whether it's work, family, or other obligations, something is going to control your time. Why not give control to the One who gifted you with your time? Creating breathing room in your schedule begins when you recognize that time is limited . . . and, therefore, valuable. Use your time wisely.

CHANGING YOUR MIND

As a reminder of the unavoidable limits on our time—and our need to

number our days—reflect on these words from Moses about this ines-

capable reality in our existence:

> *Our days may come to seventy years,*
> *or eighty, if our strength endures;*
> *yet the best of them are but trouble and sorrow,*
> *for they quickly pass, and we fly away.*
> *Psalm 90:10*

PREPARATION FOR SESSION 3

To help you prepare for Session 3, use these suggested devotions during the week leading up to your small group meeting.

Day One

Read the parable Jesus tells in Luke 16:1–9. What happens here? What are the most significant details in the story?

Day Two

In Luke 16:8–9, notice the points Jesus makes in wrapping up the parable. What is the significance of these statements? How do they relate to your own financial affairs?

Day Three

Continue in Luke 16 by reflecting on the words of Jesus in verses 10–12. What is the main lesson you take from these words? What do they have to do with your own life?

Day Four

Move on to verse 13 in Luke 16. Why do you think Jesus said, "No one *can* serve two masters" instead of, "No one *should* serve two masters"?

Day Five

Think again about Luke 16:13. Practically speaking, what are the best ways for a person to serve God instead of money?

Last Session

The right context for making wise decisions about our priorities and our use of time is the everlastingness of God and our brevity of life. We are taught in the Bible to live as if our days are numbered. We have limited time, so we need to limit how we spend it.

SESSION 3

Money

In the last session, we emphasized how our time is limited. Money is similar, yet also different. We have only so much time, and there's no way to borrow more; but we *can* borrow money. By getting deeply in debt and not being careful in managing money, we start to feel increased financial pressure so that life's no longer enjoyable. We don't even enjoy the things we bought with the money we borrowed.

Moreover—and this is huge—there's a relationship between having your financial house in order and your ability to follow Christ. It has nothing to do with giving money to the church; it has everything to do with having breathing room in your finances. That's a truth reinforced by what Jesus himself tells us about finances.

Advertisers and marketers constantly tell us that raising our standard of living means raising our quality of life. *Absolutely not true.* Those two are completely different; don't ever confuse them. You can raise your standard of living easily enough with debt; but you raise your quality of life only with *discipline*.

Creating breathing room financially may *lower* your standard of living, but it will always *raise* your quality of life.

DISCUSSION STARTER

Is God more interested in your standard of living or in your quality of life? How would you define those two concepts, and how would you describe the relationship between them as you normally think of it? As a practical matter, which is more important to you? Which one drives your life?

VIDEO OVERVIEW

For Session 3 of the DVD

When our level of spending stays below our level of income, we have breathing room financially. This is what we all desire, and when it happens, our lives are better. We sleep better, we get along better with others, we drive slower, we can pray and concentrate, and we're more generous with our time and money.

For most of us, however, our rate of spending is not less than our income. We allow any increase in income to drive up our spending. We maintain no financial margin.

Because of that, we experience financial pressure and tension, no matter how much we make.

For many of us, our spending levels exceed our incomes as we borrow our way into debt. This brings all kinds of pressure and tension, especially in our relationships. We have lives full of possessions, yet we don't enjoy them.

When there's no safe margin between income and spending, we become slaves; we've purchased and borrowed our way into slavery. We worry about money all the time. Our lives are being run by financial pressure and everything it involves.

In the New Testament, Jesus speaks extensively about money. He has said so much on the subject that we're convinced we can't be sincere followers of Jesus if our finances are out of control.

In Luke 16, Jesus tells a fascinating parable about a money manager who gets fired and then leverages his opportunities so he'll have a job afterwards. At the end of this parable, Jesus states that no one can serve two masters—that we'll hate one or the other. Then Jesus says, "You cannot serve both God and money" (Luke 16:13). Failing to understand this, we find ourselves torn between devotion to God and devotion to our possessions and wealth.

At the end of the day, we have to choose which master we'll serve.

Our financial enslavement prevents us from effectively following Jesus—for it prevents him from being our master. It bogs us down in anxiety and tension. Furthermore, it causes us to neglect our biblical calling toward serving others—because a person's financial disorder ends up making his life all about himself.

VIDEO NOTES

DISCUSSION QUESTIONS

1. Most of us can relate to the belief that *if only we had a little more income, things would be fine.* Has there ever been a period in your life when you did *not* think that way? Why do you think we're all so prone to having that perspective, no matter our income levels?

2. In what particular ways do you observe people being tempted to let money become their master, instead of God? How can that temptation be resisted?

3. What does "quality of life" look like for those who look fully to God, instead of money, as their master? What difference does this really make in life?

4. Why do you think Jesus said, "You cannot serve both God and money" instead of, "You cannot serve both God and the devil"? Does the devil represent less of a competitor for our hearts than money and possessions do? Would that be true for some but not for others?

5. For restoring financial breathing room, consider these practical steps: (1) make a commitment to achieve this breathing room; (2) set a goal for what percentage of your income you want left over after spending; (3) have an accurate, detailed grasp on every dollar you spend; (4) find ways to cut spending; (5) develop a debt-retirement plan. (For special help here, Andy recommends the book *Financial Peace Revisited* by Dave Ramsey.) What value do you see in each of these steps?

6. Jesus indicates repeatedly in the Gospels that giving an account of our financial lives will be part of the account we give to our heavenly Father at the end of our lives. What do you most want to be true about your life in this regard?

MILEPOSTS

- Standard of living does *not* equal quality of life. Achieving better quality of life may mean lowering your standard of living.

- Jesus tells us it's impossible to serve both God and money.

- Lack of financial breathing room will hold back our ability to follow Jesus.

MOVING FORWARD

Money doesn't raise your quality of life, but financial breathing room *does*. In fact, you may need a lower standard of living in order to improve your quality of life. You can't obey the teachings of Jesus without financial breathing room because he commanded us not to worry, and you'll worry a lot if you have no financial margin. Don't let your finances be your master.

CHANGING YOUR MIND

These blunt statements from Jesus are well worth our continued awareness. Reflect on them with grateful appreciation for these truths.

No one can serve two masters.
Either you will hate the one and love the other,
or you will be devoted to the one and despise the other.
You cannot serve both God and money.
Luke 16:13

PREPARATION FOR SESSION 4

To help you prepare for Session 4, use these suggested devotions during the week leading up to your small group meeting.

Day One

Read the words of the apostle Paul in Ephesians 5:21, and think about their meaning. How do you think true reverence for Christ can give us guidance and encouragement for properly submitting to one another?

Day Two

Continue in Ephesians 5 by reading Paul's words to wives in verses 22–24. What connections do you see between these words and the mutual submission and reverence for Christ that are taught in verse 21?

Day Three

Again in Ephesians 5, look at Paul's words to husbands in verses 25–32. What connections do you see between these words and the mutual submission and reverence for Christ that are taught in verse 21?

Day Four

What further New Testament teaching for wives do you see in the words of the apostle Peter in 1 Peter 3:1–2, and how does this relate to what Paul teaches women in Ephesians 5:21–24?

Day Five

What further New Testament teaching for husbands do you see in Peter's words in 1 Peter 3:7, and how does this relate to what Paul teaches men in Ephesians 5:21 and 5:25–32?

Last Session

We do not achieve a better quality of life by raising our standard of living; those two things are not connected. We *do* achieve a better quality of life when we achieve financial breathing room. And failing to achieve financial breathing room will constrict our ability to follow Jesus.

SESSION 4

Choosing to Cheat

Relationships wither and die when we're constantly living at our limits; relationships thrive only where there's *breathing room.*

As we try to get the most out of life, too many of us are squeezing in one more thing after another—until finally there's a breakdown . . . a collapse. This especially occurs in the critical relationships of our lives.

Andy and Sandra Stanley tell the story of how they came uncomfortably close to such a crisis. It happened in the mid-1990s when North Point Community Church was being launched under Andy's leadership, and the Stanleys were the parents of two small children and another on the way.

Amid this pressure at both home and work, Andy realized there simply would never be enough time to do all he needed to be doing in both places. Although Sandra is organized and gifted in leadership, and although she was fully committed to taking care of things at home while Andy pursued all that was required of him in his new ministry, there was a growing tension in their family.

The tension culminated in a long and candid conversation in which Andy asked Sandra the simple question, "What does *ideal* look like?" From this discussion came what Andy regards as the best leadership decision he ever made.

DISCUSSION STARTER

What comes to mind when you think of *submitting* to other people? What are some things that make it difficult for us to properly submit to other people?

VIDEO OVERVIEW

For Session 4 of the DVD

When we take a responsibility that we should carry and hand it to our spouses or our children, it's like handing them a big rock and telling them to hold it for a while.

We all know there are short periods in life when, because of certain constraints or pressures upon us, this may need to be done. Since our family members want to faithfully support us, they always accept these loads and carry them.

The problem comes when we leave those loads on them for an extended time. Because they're not designed or equipped to carry these responsibilities that properly belong to us, they begin to slowly wear out. Problems and tension arise.

The signs of this include our constantly repeated promises to do better, our chronic absences from important events in their lives, and our continued pointing to the future to make up for the past.

Eventually, our loved ones' mental willingness to carry our loads is overcome by their exhaustion—emotional and, in some cases, physical. That's when they drop those rocks we handed them. Reaching this stage may bring irreparable damage to the relationship—and even the end of it. It can take years to bring back the trust that was lost.

We allow this to happen because we love progress, and while we can measure progress at work, we cannot measure it at home. And when we begin to cheat what is most important—our marriages and families—for the sake of something that is secondary, there's a problem.

When Andy and Sandra faced this kind of pressure in their home,

Andy asked Sandra, "What does *ideal* look like?" Sandra said that she would reach a point in late afternoon when she was out of energy no matter how disciplined she'd been that day or how hard she'd tried to pace herself. She told Andy how helpful it would be if he could leave for home each day at four o'clock.

Knowing he had to figure out a way to create more breathing room in their marriage, Andy made the decision to do just that. In making that choice, his biggest obstacle was his fear of what others on the church staff and in the church would think.

Andy committed to giving only forty-five hours a week to his job and asked God to make the most of that.

In the New Testament, Paul tells us, "Submit to one another out of reverence for Christ" (Ephesians 5:21). This mutual submission means doing our best to ensure that the other person has what is wanted and needed.

Later in that passage, Paul says, "Husbands, love your wives, just as Christ loved the church and gave himself up for her" (Ephesians 5:25). Husbands follow Christ's example when they seek the well-being of their wives more than their own ambitions and desires for progress.

VIDEO NOTES

_____

_____

_____

_____

_____

_____

_____

_____

_____

_____

_____

_____

_____

_____

_____

_____

_____

_____

_____

DISCUSSION QUESTIONS

1. In your significant relationships, what are the unique roles you're called to? What are your primary responsibilities and affections in those roles?

2. In your significant relationships, what are the biggest things you're trusting God for? What are the biggest things you *want* to trust God for? In what ways does fear enter in and create obstacles to that trust on your part?

3. How much do you agree with this statement: You'll never be happier than the relationships you have with those who are most precious to you? To what degree have you already seen and experienced this to be true?

4. When it comes to your relationships, how firmly do you see God as being in control of them?

5. What is your best understanding of *mutual submission* in relationships, as taught in Scripture (Ephesians 5:21)? What does this look like in your most significant relationships?

6. What are some practical ways you can create more breathing room in your most important relationships?

MILEPOSTS

- Relationships wither and die when we're constantly living at our limits; relationships thrive only where there's breathing room.

- The Bible teaches us that *mutual submission* is a relational essential. We must pursue what is best for one another at the expense of our own preferences and desires.

- Husbands, in relating to their wives, are commanded to follow Christ's example of sacrificial love for the church.

MOVING FORWARD

There may not be enough time to accomplish everything you want to get done or everything that culture tells you must get done. You may have to "cheat" on something. But *where* will you cheat? *Whom* will you cheat? In your desire to get the most out of life, remember to first stay loyal to those you *love*—those whom God has given and called you to love.

CHANGING YOUR MIND

This New Testament command reminds us of a dynamic principle in

every healthy relationship that pleases and honors God.

Submit to one another
out of reverence for Christ.
Ephesians 5:21

BREATHING | ROOM

The space between our current
pace and our limits

LEADER GUIDE

Leader Guide

LEADING YOURSELF

Leading others begins with leading yourself. You're in a unique position to influence the lives of the people in your group. But you have to lead yourself first.

Depend on God.

Self-leading begins with being fully dependent on God. The best leaders have learned how to follow God. They know they are *always* under his authority. Keep in mind that you're a steward of what God has entrusted to you—beginning with yourself. Your gifts don't belong to you and they aren't there to serve you. God has given them to you so you can use them to serve him.

Most important, in order to lead yourself well, you must follow the Holy Spirit. Learn how to let the Spirit lead you. Don't get out in front of him. This can be tricky (you are, after all, a leader). But it's important to remember that God is in charge, not you.

Be self-aware.

Leading yourself involves knowing yourself. You should be a lifelong student of you. If you can't currently answer the following questions, start moving in the direction where you can.

- *What is your personality type?*

- *What are your top three spiritual gifts?*

- *What energizes you?*

- *What drains you?*

- *How do you best connect with God?*

In addition to being a lifelong student of yourself, you need to have people in your life who know your weaknesses and struggles and who love you enough to point them out to you. We all have imperfections we can't see. The remedy is a trusted circle of friends to hold us accountable. Leaning into other people isn't enough, though. On a regular basis, you need to ask God to reveal your faults, to refine you, and to make you more and more like Jesus.[1]

Be intentional.

To lead yourself well, you have to be intentional—you have to *do something*. All self-leaders do five things:

1. Begin with the end in mind. Self-leaders have a vision for the kind of people they want to be and they pursue that vision.

2. Actively learn. Self-leaders recognize that they're responsible for their spiritual development. They explore and discover. They're curious.

3. Practice rest. Self-leaders make time to reflect and recharge.

[1]Psalm 139:23–24

They maintain a sustainable pace.

4. Pursue health. Self-leaders take the necessary steps to become or remain physically, emotionally, and relationally healthy.

5. Lead from the inside out. Self-leaders recognize they can never rise above the limits of their own character. They cultivate integrity and moral authority by maintaining harmony between what they say and how they live.

LEADING THE DISCUSSION
So, you're the leader . . .

No doubt you have some mental pictures of what it will look like to lead—what you will say and how group members will respond. Before you get too far into the planning process, there are some things you should know about leading a small group discussion.

Cultivate discussion.

It's easy to think that a group meeting lives or dies on the quality of your ideas. That's not true. It's the ideas of everyone in the group that make a small group meeting successful. Your role is to create an environment in which people feel safe to share their thoughts. That's how relationships will grow and thrive among your group members.

Here's a basic truth about spiritual growth within the context of community: the study materials aren't as important as the relationships through which those materials take practical shape in the lives of the group members. The more meaningful the relationships, the more meaningful the study. The best materials in the world won't change lives in a sterile environment.

Point to the material.

A good host or hostess creates an environment where people can connect relationally. He or she knows when to help guests connect and when to stay out of the way when those connections are happening organically. As a small group leader, sometimes you'll simply read a discussion question and invite everyone to respond. The conversation will take care of itself. At other times, you may need to encourage group members to share their ideas. Remember, some of the best insights will come from the people in your group. Go with the flow, but be ready to nudge the conversation in the right direction when necessary.

Depart from the material.

We've carefully designed this study for your small group. We've written the materials and designed the questions to elicit the kinds of conversations we think will be most helpful to your group members.

That doesn't mean you should stick rigidly to the materials. Knowing when to depart from them is more art than science, but no one knows more about your group than you do.

The stories, questions, and exercises are here to provide a framework for exploration. But different groups have different chemistries and different motivations. Sometimes the best way to start a small group discussion is to ask, "Does anyone have a personal insight you'd like to share from this week's material?" Then sit back and listen.

Stay on track.

This is the flip side to the previous point. There's an art to facilitating an engaging conversation. While you want to leave space for group members to think through the discussion, you also need to keep your objectives in mind. Make sure the discussion is contributing to the bottom line for the week. Don't let the discussion veer off into tangents. Interject politely in order to refocus the group.

Pray.

This is the most important thing you can do as a leader. The best leaders get out of God's way and let him communicate *through* them.

Remember: books don't teach God's Word; neither do sermons or discussion groups. God speaks into the hearts of men and women. Prayer is a vital part of communicating with him.

Pray for your group members. Pray for your own leadership. Pray that God is not only present at your group meetings, but is directing them.

We hope you find these suggestions helpful, and we hope you enjoy leading this study. You will find additional guidelines and suggestions for each session in the Leader Guide notes that follow.

Leader Guide
Session Notes

SESSION 1 — EX-SQUEEZE YOURSELF

Bottom Line

We all need to recognize that we have limits, and we should be clearly aware of what those limits are. We also must realize that fear often lies at the root of our refusal to live within our limits. The result is a tragic loss of peace and breathing room.

Discussion Starter

Use the "Discussion Starter" printed in Session 1 of the Participant Guide to "break the ice" and to help everyone think about the overall dynamics of calm order versus out-of-control disorder in the most important aspects of our lives.

Notes for Discussion Questions

1. **As you observe your own life or the lives of those around you, when people operate very close to their limits, how does it affect them physically, emotionally, mentally, and relationally?**

    Allow plenty of time to discuss these aspects of the negative impact of having no breathing room.

2. **Where do you feel you need some breathing room? In what areas could you be living dangerously close to your limits, and how is this affecting you? What are the forces at work in your life that tend to push you toward these limits? To what degree is *fear* involved in this?**

    Share your own honest response here, which will be the best encouragement for thorough, honest answers from the rest of the group.

3. **How fully conscious are you of the fact that God knows your personal limits in every area of life? How does this fact affect your ability to trust him?**

    Again, your own genuine response here will help open up everyone else in the group to share candidly.

4. **Jesus reminds us (in Mark 2:27) that God gave the Sabbath for man's benefit. In Exodus 20:8–11, look at how the Sabbath is described in this listing of God's Ten Commandments. What does this reveal about God's care for humanity and his**

understanding of humanity? What else does it reveal about his character?

Help the group imagine what these guidelines from God would mean in the agrarian culture that Israel would experience in the Promised Land. Help them realize God's never-ending love and concern for the poor and disadvantaged in any and every culture.

5. **Look also at the provision God made for his people in Leviticus 19:9–10 (and extended further in Deuteronomy 24:19–22). What does this provision reveal about God's character? What practical benefit would this have provided? How does the principle here relate to the concept of finding breathing room in our lives today?**

Talk about God's command to not harvest all of a farmer's crop, but to share the abundance with those less fortunate (*gleaning*). This concept applies to us having enough breathing room in our finances to be generous with others, allowing us to experience the blessing that comes with our generosity.

6. **Finally, look at the words of Jesus in Matthew 6:25–33. What good reasons for trusting God do you find here? How does this passage expose our fears? In the practical matters of life, what does trusting God really look like, according to the guidelines given in this passage?**

The key purpose here is to help everyone clearly grasp the love and trustworthiness of God as expressed in these words of Jesus.

Moving Forward

The goal here is to help everyone in the group face up to his or her limits and fully accept responsibility for stepping back from living on the dangerous edge of those limits. As you close, ask each person in the group to pray a one-sentence prayer that thanks God for caring for us enough to want our lives to have breathing room.

Preparation for Session 2

Remember to point out the brief daily devotions that group members can complete and that will help stimulate discussion in your next session. These devotions will enable everyone to dig into the Bible and start wrestling with the topics that will come up next time.

SESSION 2 — TIME

Bottom Line

Our time is limited, but we so often fail to recognize that basic truth and to let that influence how we set priorities and make time-use decisions. We must learn to live each day in light of God's everlastingness and our own brevity of life.

Discussion Starter

Use the "Discussion Starter" printed in Session 2 of the Participant Guide to "break the ice"—and to help everyone see the critical importance of being actively aware of our own coming deaths—something our culture actively resists.

Notes for Discussion Questions

1. **What are the biggest lessons you've learned about spending time wisely?**

   Most people can look back in their own experience and recognize how "wasteful" wasted time really is. Encourage them to draw out these lessons and make the most of them. Allow each person in the group to articulate this as fully as possible.

2. **To what degree do you view time as your most treasured asset? On a practical level, what does it look like for a person to truly regard time as his or her most treasured asset?**

   Encourage not only recognition of the precious value of time, but also gratitude and appreciation toward God for giving our time to us.

3. **What are the most significant pressures you face as you try to make wise decisions about your use of time? How can you counteract these pressures?**

   Let your own honest answers here lead the way for others. Think especially of what you most want God to accomplish in your life.

4.   **One recent researcher (Bronnie Ware of Australia, in her book *The Top Five Regrets of the Dying* published in 2012) identified these top two deathbed regrets: (1) "I wish I'd had the courage to live a life true to myself, not the life others expected of me," and (2) "I wish I hadn't worked so hard" (this one being especially common among men). How would you evaluate your life in those two areas? How likely is it that either of those regrets will be in your mind as you lie upon your deathbed?**

This question could lead to an opportune moment for bringing in the power of the gospel—power to not only redeem us from the regrets in our pasts, but also to transform our current lives as we experience God's grace, healing, and help.

5.   **How fully does your current schedule allow you to pursue what you know is truly most important in your life? Who or what do you need to *add* to your schedule, or give *more* time to? Who or what do you need to *remove* from your schedule, or give less time to?**

Share your own honest response here, encouraging everyone to do the same.

6.   **When you give serious thought to making your schedule align more closely with your deepest values and priorities, what fears or anxieties come to mind?**

Most of us need lots of help in becoming more honest with ourselves, so allow plenty of time for the discussion here.

Moving Forward

The goal here is to help group members face up to the brevity of life and their coming deaths, and to commit to making time-use decisions based on that perspective—in light of the everlastingness of God. As you close, ask each person in the group to pray a sentence prayer that gives thanks to God for the time he has given us.

Preparation for Session 3

Remember to point out the brief daily devotions that group members can complete and that will help stimulate discussion in your next session. These devotions will enable everyone to dig into the Bible and start wrestling with the topics that will come up next time.

SESSION 3 — MONEY

Bottom Line

We must recognize that we can never improve our quality of life by pursuing a higher standard of living, especially when that means abandoning our financial breathing room and financial peace. When we put ourselves in that bondage, we make ourselves unavailable for serving Jesus as our Lord and Master.

Discussion Starter

Use the "Discussion Starter" printed in Session 3 of the Participant Guide to "break the ice"—and to help everyone see the critical difference between these two concepts: standard of living and quality of life.

Notes for Discussion Questions

1. **Most of us can relate to the belief that *if only we had a little more income, things would be fine*. Has there ever been a period in your life when you did *not* think that way? Why do you think we're all so prone to having that perspective, no matter our income levels?**
Most of us have times when we tend to feel this way. Encourage honest discussion about it. Help guide the group's awareness toward the truth that this feeling actually has nothing to do with how much income we're receiving.

2. **In what particular ways do you observe people being tempted to let money become their master, instead of God? How can that temptation be resisted?**
Help guide the discussion toward the truth of God's available help for us when we battle this temptation.

3. **What does "quality of life" look like for those who look fully to God, instead of money, as their master? What difference does this really make in life?**
Help guide the discussion toward the truth that *relationships*—with God and with others—are the only source of true "quality of life."

4. **Why do you think Jesus said, "You cannot serve both God and money" instead of, "You cannot serve both God and the devil"? Does the devil represent less of a competitor for our hearts than money and possessions do? Would that be true for some but not for others?**

This question could spark some interesting discussion. Help the group see that anything we devote our lives to will usurp God's rightful place in our hearts.

5. **For restoring financial breathing room, consider these practical steps: (1) make a commitment to achieve this breathing room; (2) set a goal for what percentage of your income you want left over after spending; (3) have an accurate, detailed grasp on every dollar you spend; (4) find ways to cut spending; (5) developing a debt-retirement plan. (For special help here, Andy recommends the book *Financial Peace Revisited* by Dave Ramsey.) What value do you see in each of these steps?**

    Allow plenty of time for this, since for many of us, specific and practical help is needed to escape the bondage of debt and be restored to financial peace and breathing room.

6. **Jesus indicates repeatedly in the Gospels that giving an account of our financial lives will be part of the account we give to our heavenly Father at the end of our lives. What do you most want to be true about your life in this regard?**

    Again, this could be an opportune moment for bringing in the power of the gospel—power to not only redeem us from mistakes and regrets in our pasts, but also to transform our current lives through the Holy Spirit's presence so that we better obey the financial guidelines given by Jesus. Then, in the end, we can hear the Lord say to us, "Well done, good and faithful servant! You have been faithful with a few things; I will put you in charge of many things. Come and share your master's happiness!" (Matthew 25:21). Ask each group memeber to offer a sentence prayer that recognizes our dependence on God and his grace and truth.

Moving Forward

The goal here is to help everyone in the group commit to seek and pursue personal financial breathing room—even if that means a decline in standard of living. Take time to pray as a group, giving thanks to God for his fatherly care for each one of us.

Preparation for Session 4

Remember to point out the brief daily devotions that the group members can complete that will help stimulate discussion in your next session. These devotions will enable everyone to dig into the Bible and start wrestling with the topics that will come up next time.

SESSION 4 — CHOOSING TO CHEAT

Bottom Line

We can't "do it all," so we have we have to "cheat" somewhere—but the place to cheat is never at home, in our most significant relationships. Those relationships will always require our mutual submission and sacrificial love.

Discussion Starter

Use the "Discussion Starter" printed in Session 4 of the Participant Guide to "break the ice"—and to help everyone get a clearer picture of what mutual submission means from a biblical perspective.

Notes for Discussion Questions

1. **In your significant relationships, what are the unique roles you're called to? What are your primary responsibilities and affections in those roles?**

    Help guide the group's awareness, especially toward their marriage and family roles.

2. **In your significant relationships, what are the biggest things you're trusting God for? What are the biggest things you *want* to trust God for? In what ways does fear enter in and create obstacles to that trust on your part?**

    Allow plenty of time to reflect and respond to this. Help the group realize that none of us wants to look back someday and say with regret, "I wonder what God would have done back then if I had trusted him, if I hadn't allowed fear to control me."

3. **How much do you agree with this statement: You'll never be happier than the relationships you have with those who are most precious to you? To what degree have you already seen and experienced this to be true?**

    Help everyone realize the crucial importance of this truth. Help point the group toward gratitude and appreciation for God's gift of relationships.

4.   **When it comes to your relationships, how firmly do you see God as being in control of them?**
       Encourage the group to grant God full ownership of all their relationships, so that he alone has final authority over how we invest in those relationships and over what they mean to us.

5.   **What is your best understanding of *mutual submission* in relationships, as taught in Scripture (Ephesians 5:21)? What does this look like in your most significant relationships?**
       Allow plenty of time to help the group see the critical importance of yielding our own preferences and "rights" for the sake of loving and helping others.

6.   **What are some practical ways you can create more breathing room in your most important relationships?**
       Together, look for ways to overcome your self-centered temptation to think you've already done "enough," and to instead be constantly sensitive and aware of new opportunities and privileges to serve others.

Moving Forward

The goal here is to help all group members renew their personal commitments to their relationships at home. Take time to pray together in grateful acknowledgment of the significant opportunity for *breathing room* that each of us has been granted by our heavenly Father *for our good.*